CIMA REVISION CARDS

Enterprise Management

David R. Harris

Managerial Level Paper E2

ELSEVIER

CIMA PUBLISHING

AMSTERDAM • BOSTON • HEIDELBERG • LONDON • NEW YORK • OXFOR
PARIS • SAN DIEGO • SAN FRANCISCO • SINGAPORE • SYDNEY • TOKYO

CIMA Publishing is an imprint of Elsevier
Linacre House, Jordan Hill, Oxford OX2 8DP
30, Corporate Drive, Burlington, MA 01803

British Library Cataloguing in Publication Data
A catalogue record for this book is available from the British Library

Library of Congress Cataloging in Publication Data
A catalog record for this book is available from the Library of Congress

ISBN: 978-1-85617-739-9

For information on all CIMA publications visit our website at www.elsevierdirect.com

Printed and bound in Great Britain

09 10 11   11 10 9 8 7 6 5 4 3 2 1

Working together to grow
libraries in developing countries

www.elsevier.com | www.bookaid.org | www.sabre.org

ELSEVIER   BOOK AID
International   Sabre Foundation

Welcome to CIMA's Official Revision Cards. These cards have been designed to:

- Save you time by summarising the syllabus in a concise form
- Jog your memory through the use of diagrams and bullet points
- Follow the structure of the CIMA Official Learning Systems
- Refer to relevant questions found within the Preparing for the Examination section of the Learning System
- Provide you with plenty of exams tips and hints

Ensure exam success by revising with the only revision cards endorsed by CIMA.

TABLE OF CONTENTS

SYLLABUS STRUCTURE AND ASSESSMENT STRATEGY

The syllabus comprises the following topics and study weightings:

A	Strategic Management and Assessing the Competitive Environment	30%
B	Project Management	40%
C	Management of Relationships	30%

There will be a written examination paper of three hours, plus 20 minutes of pre-examination question paper reading time. The examination paper will have the following sections:

Section A – 50 marks

Five compulsory medium answer questions, each worth 10 marks. Short scenarios may be given, to which some or all questions relate.

Section B – 50 marks

One or two compulsory questions. Short scenarios may be given, to which questions relate.

The Nature of Strategic Management

Topics

- What is strategy?
- The rational model of strategy development
- Alternatives to the rational model
- Formal business strategy
- Resource-based vs. positioning views

- Stakeholders
- Mission and objective setting
- Terminology
- Critical success factor analysis
- Competing objectives
- Tools for strategic analysis

Key learning system questions

1

What is strategy?

Common themes in strategy

⇨ It is about the purpose and long-term objectives of the business

⇨ It is concerned with meeting the challenges from the firm's business environment

⇨ It involves using the firm's resources effectively, and building on its strategies to meet environmental challenges

⇨ It is ultimately about delivering value to the people who depend on the firm, its stakeholders, such as customers and shareholders

Definitions

Strategy – a course of action, including the specification of resources required, to achieve a specific objective

Strategic plan – a statement of long-term goals along with a definition of the strategies which will ensure the achievement of these goals

Study tip

Many exam questions will look at the common themes opposite. Make sure you understand the issues involved

What is strategy?

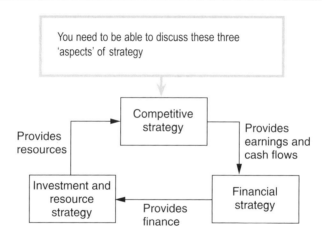

What is strategy?

What is strategy?

Corporate strategy

⇨ Acquisitions, mergers, sell-offs or closure of strategic business units
⇨ Conduct of relations with key external stakeholders
⇨ Decisions to enter new markets or embrace new technologies
⇨ Corporate policies on public image, employment practices or Information Systems

Business strategy

⇨ Marketing issues such as product, price, promotion, place
⇨ Decisions on production technology
⇨ Staffing decisions

Functional strategy

⇨ Long-term management policies for individual functional areas (e.g. sales, production)

These are just examples of the three levels of strategy. You need to be able to identify others in a scenario and discuss them

The rational model of strategy development

Make sure you understand, and can reproduce, this diagram

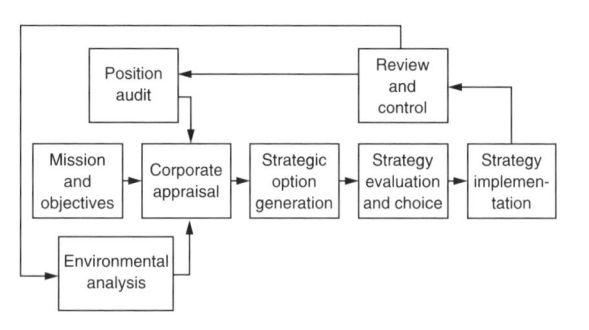

The rational model of strategy development

Stages in the rational model

⇨ Mission and objectives
⇨ Position audit
⇨ Environmental analysis
⇨ Corporate appraisal
⇨ Strategic option generation
⇨ Strategy evaluation and choice
⇨ Strategy implementation
⇨ Review and control

Study tip

You need to know the issues that arise at each of these stages. Exam questions might ask about one or more

And also

You might link the 'strategic planning tools' to each of the stages of the rational model, for example PEST analysis and the competitive forces model are both used in environmental analysis

Alternatives to the rational model

Criticisms of the rational model

⇨ Organisations are incapable of having objectives
⇨ Senior management should not be the only people involved in setting strategy
⇨ In reality, strategy setting is not a simple, step-by-step process
⇨ The strategies firms follow are not the same as the ones they set out in their plans
⇨ Strategy is not something decided in advance by managers
⇨ Strategy should not be a rational process

Alternatives

Definitions

Emergent strategies – patterns or consistencies realised despite, or in the absence of, intentions

Logical incrementalism – a manager maps where he or she wants the organisation to go, and then proceeds towards it in small steps, being prepared to adapt if the environment changes or support is not forthcoming

This is sometimes known as 'muddling through,' though logical incrementalism can be a deliberate strategic approach

Formal business strategy

Features

⇨ Designated team
⇨ Formal information system for strategy
⇨ Collective decision taking
⇨ A communication and implementation process
⇨ Regular review

Benefits

⇨ Avoids short-termism
⇨ Helps issue identification
⇨ Goal congruence
⇨ Improved stakeholder perception
⇨ Basis for strategic control
⇨ Develops potential and ensures continuity

Drawbacks

⇨ Not dynamic
⇨ Not radical or innovative
⇨ Difficult to implement
⇨ Loss of entrepreneurism
⇨ Impossible in uncertain environment
⇨ Too expensive and complex for small businesses

Resource-based vs. positioning views

Positioning view

Believes that supernormal profits result from:
⇨ High market share,
⇨ A differentiated product or
⇨ Low costs

Resource-based view

Believes that supernormal profits result from the possession of unique skills or resources, and that the positioning view is invalid because:
⇨ Competitive advantage is not sustainable
⇨ Environments are too dynamic to position in
⇨ It is easier to change the environment than to change the firm

However, the resource-based view has been criticised because:
⇨ It conflicts with the conventional product/market based view of strategy
⇨ It challenges the rational model
⇨ It conflicts with the notion of network organisations, as managers would not wish to share core competences

Study tip

This debate is quite examinable. Make sure you understand the issues

Stakeholders

Definition

Stakeholders – groups or individuals having a legitimate interest in the activities of an organisation

Study tip

Make sure you understand, and can apply, the Mendelow matrix. It is a key stakeholder management tool

Stakeholders include

⇨ Shareholders and other investors
⇨ Management
⇨ Employees
⇨ Customers
⇨ Suppliers
⇨ Local community
⇨ Government

Level of interest

	Low	High
Low	A Minimal effort	B Keep informed
High	C Keep satisfied	D Key players

Power

Mission and objective setting

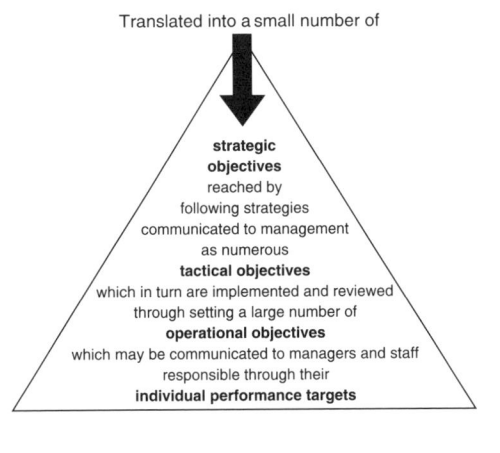

Translated into a small number of

strategic
objectives
reached by
following strategies
communicated to management
as numerous
tactical objectives
which in turn are implemented and reviewed
through setting a large number of
operational objectives
which may be communicated to managers and staff
responsible through their
individual performance targets

Study tip

Make sure you understand, and can apply, this diagram

Terminology

Term	Definition	Personal example
Mission	Overriding purpose in line with the values and expectations of stakeholders	Be healthy and fit
Vision or strategic intent	Desired future state: the aspiration of the organisation	To run the London marathon
Goal	General statement of aim or purpose	Lose weight and strengthen muscle
Strategies	Long-term direction	Associate with a collaborative network (e.g. join a running club), exercise regularly, compete marathons, stick to appropriate diet
Objective	Quantification (if possible) or more precise statement of the goal	Lose 10 pounds by 1 September and run the marathon in 18 months time

Mission

⇨ Provides a basis for planning decisions
⇨ Assists in translating purpose into objectives
⇨ Encourages goal congruence
⇨ Supports ethical behaviour
⇨ Improves understanding of external stakeholders

Objectives

Should be 'SMART':
⇨ Specific
⇨ Measurable
⇨ Attainable
⇨ Relevant
⇨ Time-bound

Study tip

These topics are all very examinable

Remember that objectives perform five functions ('PRIME'):

Planning

Responsibility

Integration

Motivation

Evaluation

Critical success factor analysis

Critical success factor (CSF) – the limited number of areas in which results, if they are satisfactory, will enable successful competitive performance

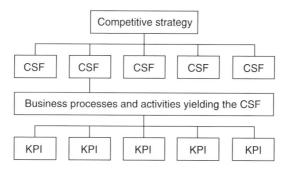

Competing objectives

Conflict occurs

⇨ Between financial and non-financial objectives
⇨ Between profit maximisation and other goals
⇨ Between the objectives of different stakeholders

Conflict solutions

⇨ Prioritisation
⇨ Weighting and scoring
⇨ Creation of composite measures
⇨ Satisficing
⇨ Sequential attention
⇨ Side payments
⇨ Exercise of power

Study tip

Identify your own specific examples of
stakeholder conflict

Tools for strategic analysis

The value chain

⇨ Inbound logistics
⇨ Operations
⇨ Outbound logistics
⇨ Marketing and sales
⇨ Service
⇨ Procurement
⇨ Technology development
⇨ Human resource management
⇨ Firm infrastructure

PEST analysis

⇨ Political
⇨ Economic
⇨ Social
⇨ Technological

SWOT analysis

⇨ Strengths
⇨ Weaknesses
⇨ Opportunities
⇨ Threats

Study tip

You need to be able to draw the diagram, explain the model and apply the framework to organisations described in question scenarios

The Competitive Environment

Topics

- The importance of the business environment: Porter and PEST
- Causes of environmental uncertainty
- Competitor analysis
- The global economic environment
- National competitive advantage
- Sources of information

The importance of the business environment: Porter and PEST

Definition

Environmental impact assessment – A study which considers potential environmental effects during the planning phase before an investment is made or an operation started

Environmental segmentation

⇨ Think of the environment as everything outside the firm and its control
⇨ We use two main models – Porter Five forces analysis and PEST

Porter's five forces are

⇨ Rivalry amongst existing firms
⇨ Bargaining power of buyers
⇨ Bargaining power of suppliers
⇨ Threat of new entrants
⇨ Threat of substitute products or services

Barriers to entry

⇨ Economies of scale
⇨ Product differentiation
⇨ Capital requirements
⇨ Switching costs
⇨ Access to distribution channels
⇨ Cost advantages independent of scale
⇨ Government policy

The importance of the business environment: Porter and PEST

PEST analysis – factors are

⇨ Political / legal influences
⇨ Economic factors and influences
⇨ Social values and demographic factors
⇨ Technological change and factors

Debate about PEST

⇨ Some authors advocate PESTEL where the 'extra' letters separate out ecological and legal factors
⇨ In real companies it doesn't really matter which acronym is used – but it does matter that the company does perform environmental screening
⇨ In real life it is difficult to categorise factors as fitting purely into one of the categories of the model

Evaluation of environmental segment models

⇨ They will encourage management to consider a wide range of environmental factors

⇨ They allow the division of work between different groups

⇨ They provide a common language for discussion

⇨ They can assist in providing insight into strategic issues

⇨ But they don't reflect reality

⇨ But they ignore the fact that the environment is a complex adaptive system with many interdependencies

⇨ But they may cause management to overlook networks

⇨ They can involve a lot of work

Study tip

⇨ Do not just learn one model – you may be asked to compare them

⇨ Do make sure that you are aware of the kind of factors that could arise under each category factor

⇨ Do practice environmental screening yourself by looking at an industry (or industries) of your choice and see what a company could gain by being more aware of the factors that could bring about change and the elements that make the industry more or less competitive

⇨ Whilst you are considering environmental analysis you should also think about political risk at both the country and industry level

Causes of environmental uncertainty

Definition

Uncertainty – The inability to predict the outcome from an activity due to a lack of information about the required input / output relationships or about the environment within which the activity takes place

Impact of uncertainty

⇨ Reduces planning horizon
⇨ Discourages deliberate strategies
⇨ Increases information needs and perceived information needs
⇨ Can lead to conservative strategies

Uncertainty caused by

⇨ Complexity – the increasing number of variables that impact upon the firm (and how difficult they are to understand)

⇨ Interaction of the variables – the idea of complex adaptive systems
⇨ Dynamism – the rate of change in the variables that impact upon the firm. Our assumptions are soon out of date. This has occurred because of, amongst other things, shortening product life cycles and swifter communications (the diffusion of knowledge)

Study tip

You will certainly be presented with uncertainty in examination questions please make sure that you can advise the decision makers in the question how to deal with it

Competitor analysis

Definition

Competitor analysis – The systematic review of all available information (marketing, production, financial, etc.) on the activities of competitors in order to gain a competitive advantage

Competitor threat

1. Number of rivals and the extent of differentiation in the market
2. Entry and mobility barriers
3. Cost structure
4. Degree of vertical integration

Purpose of competitor analysis

⇨ To help understand our competitive advantage/ disadvantage relative to competition
⇨ To forecast competitors future strategies and how to counteract them
⇨ To give an informed basis for the construction of the firms' strategies to gain or sustain competitive advantage
⇨ To assist with the forecasting of the returns on strategic investments when deciding between alternative options
⇨ To forecast competitors likely reactions to the firms strategic decisions

Competitor analysis

Levels of competitor

⇨ Brand
⇨ Industry
⇨ Form
⇨ Generic

Information that should be gathered

To include: products and services, marketing, human resources, operations, management profiles, sociopolitical, technology, organisational structure, competitive intelligence capacity, strategy, customer value analysis, financial, cost structures

Study tip

Make sure that you are able to discuss the advantages and disadvantages of competitor analysis – don't forget it is strongly linked to Five forces analysis. In scenario questions you should be looking for clues to the industry structure and therefore, the nature of the competition that a firm is likely to experience in that industry

Competitor analysis

Sources of data

⇨ From partnership agreements
⇨ Physical analysis of competitors' products
⇨ Banks and financial markets
⇨ Ex-employees of competitors
⇨ Generalisation from own cost base
⇨ Industrial experts and consultants
⇨ Physical observations of their operations
⇨ Published financial statements
⇨ Competitor press releases
⇨ Trade and financial media coverage

⇨ Inspection of wage rates in job adverts
⇨ Availability and cost of their finance
⇨ Characteristics of the market segments they serve
⇨ The work methods they employ

Study tip

When presented with a question that looks for sources of information, check to see if the question ask you to relate it to the scenario in the question – if it does don't just put down a wish list, focus on the industry in question

The global economic environment

The economic environment

We need to consider the economic environment at two levels:

1. The global economic environment
2. The operational economic environment in the country or countries in which the firm operates

The global economic environment

⇨ An important trend is internationalisation – the extension of trade across national borders
⇨ A further important trend is globalisation – the functional integration of internationally dispersed activities

Globalisation is being brought about by

⇨ Extension of supply chains across national boundaries
⇨ Changing patterns of foreign direct investment (FDI)
⇨ The creation of supranational organisations
⇨ Economic changes being driven by technology
⇨ The spread of multinational enterprises
⇨ Transfer of particular industries across national boundaries causing the spread of dominant cultures and lifestyles

National competitive advantage

Porter's diamond

Attempts to answer the questions:

1. Why do certain nations have so many successful international firms?
2. How do these firms sustain superior performance in a global market?
3. What are the implications of this for government policy and competitive strategy?

The elements of success are

⇨ Demand conditions in the home market
⇨ Related and supporting industries
⇨ Factor conditions
⇨ The firm's structure, strategy and rivalry
⇨ The role of government and chance

Porter's strategic prescriptions

⇨ The firm should identify which home country clusters will give an advantage – either cost or differentiation

⇨ If those advantages are world class they should compete on a global basis

⇨ If those advantages are not world class they should compete locally in an appropriate niche market

Sources of information

Gathering environmental information can be done at different levels of intensity and levels within the organisation

1. In addition to their operational duties, line management should have the responsibility of environmental scanning in the medium term
2. Those responsible for the strategic planning of the organisation should have the task of gathering information with a longer time horizon
3. There may be 'business intelligence units' whose specific responsibility is scanning

Importance of environmental scanning

⇨ Provides a base of (hopefully) objective qualitative information
⇨ Assists firm in seizing opportunities and protecting against threats
⇨ Encourages sensitivity to changing needs of society and hence customers
⇨ Provides essential information for strategic planning process
⇨ Provides intellectual stimulation for strategists
⇨ Provides a broad-based education and awareness for managers
⇨ Creates a good impression both inside and outside the firm

Categorisation of sources

Study tip

⇨ Primary sources such as annual reports, transcript services, government surveys and departments, newspapers, magazines and journals and patent registrations

⇨ Secondary sources such as directories and yearbooks, market research reviews and reports, current awareness services, specialist databases, reports from government committees and conference reports

⇨ Computer-based information (of increasing importance), online data bases of professional journals and academic institutions

⇨ The Internet in particular

Throughout this chapter we have discussed the importance of information external to the company and how it can be gathered. Many companies do not take this area as seriously as they should for a variety of reasons – too much effort, too hard, too complicated are amongst the most common quoted

Contemporary Thinking on Strategy

Topics

- Trends in management and structure
- New patterns of employment
- Ecological perspective and transaction cost theory
- Social responsibility
- Ethics

Key learning system question

Changes in the business environment

⇨ Multinational organisations
⇨ Saturated markets
⇨ Global markets
⇨ Deregulation
⇨ Increasing competition
⇨ Flatter, leaner organisations
⇨ Network organisations
⇨ Global and international structures

Network organisations

⇨ Contract staffing
⇨ Use of specific capital assets
⇨ Outsourcing production/service delivery
⇨ Reliance on external referrals

Study tip

These issues are more likely to form the background to a question, rather than be the topic of the question itself. Think about the impact of these issues on the organisation

New patterns of employment

Impact of flexibility on employment

⇨ Contract-based flexibility
⇨ Time-based flexibility
⇨ Job-based flexibility
⇨ Skill-based flexibility
⇨ Organisation-based flexibility
⇨ Pay-based flexibility

Flexible time arrangements

⇨ Flexible working hours
⇨ Compressed hours
⇨ Job sharing

Shamrock organisation (Handy)

⇨ Core (indispensable people)
⇨ Interface (flexible labour force)
⇨ Suppliers (outsourced key services)

Study tip

Handy's shamrock structure is just one example of how a flexible organisation might work, you should think of examples where this type of structure would be appropriate

Ecological perspective and transaction cost theory

Areas to be monitored

⇨ Production
⇨ Environmental auditing
⇨ Ecological approach
⇨ Quality
⇨ Accounting
⇨ Economic

Transaction cost theory

⇨ Bounded rationality
⇨ Opportunistic behaviour
⇨ Asset specificity
    ⇨ Site
    ⇨ Physical
    ⇨ Human
    ⇨ Dedicated
    ⇨ Brand
    ⇨ Temporal

Transaction costs

⇨ Negotiation costs
⇨ Monitoring costs
⇨ Legal costs
⇨ Penalty costs

Social responsibility

Definition

Social responsibility – taking more than just the immediate interests of the shareholders into account when making a business decision

Issues

⇨ Pollution
⇨ Safety
⇨ Discrimination
⇨ Renewable resources
⇨ Social desirability
⇨ Bio-degradable products and packaging

Conflicts between social responsibility and shareholder wealth

⇨ Additional costs
⇨ Reduced revenues
⇨ Diversion of shareholder funds
⇨ Waste of management time

Benefits of social responsibility

⇨ Become a sustainable enterprise
⇨ Attract socially conscious investors
⇨ Attract socially conscious customers
⇨ Improve relations with government and regulators
⇨ Reduced stress and improved morale

Definition

Ethics – issues of moral rightness and wrongness of decisions and actions

Ethical issues

⇨ Advertising
⇨ Pay and working conditions
⇨ Exploitation of countries or peoples
⇨ Product effects
⇨ Oppressive governments
⇨ Closures and redundancies

Topics

- Definition and characteristics
- The project life cycle
- The iterative approach
- Other frameworks
- Why projects fail
- Strategy and scope
- Project manager – roles and skills
- Problems with teams
- Stakeholders and matrix structures

Key learning system question

Definition and characteristics

Definition

Project – a human activity that achieves a clear objective against a time scale

Study tip

You need to be able to explain these characteristics and to identify them for real projects

Characteristics

⇨ Stakeholders
⇨ Uniqueness
⇨ Objectives
⇨ Resources
⇨ Schedules
⇨ Quality
⇨ Uncertainty
⇨ Finiteness
⇨ Change

The project life cycle

⇨ Identification of need
⇨ Development of solution
⇨ Implementation
⇨ Completion

Problems

⇨ Too slow
⇨ Lack of user/customer involvement
⇨ Assumes requirements are certain before the start

The iterative approach

⇨ Use for smaller projects
⇨ Use where needs are uncertain
⇨ Involve users
⇨ Create a 'predictive model'
⇨ Try out the solution
⇨ Repeat the life cycle until everyone is happy
⇨ Reduces risk

4-D

⇨ Discover
⇨ Dream
⇨ Design
⇨ Deliver

The 5 process areas

⇨ Initiating
⇨ Planning
⇨ Executing
⇨ Controlling
⇨ Closing

The 9 knowledge areas

⇨ Integration
⇨ Scope
⇨ Time
⇨ Cost
⇨ Quality
⇨ Resource
⇨ Communication
⇨ Risk
⇨ Procurement

Why projects fail

⇨ Time/resource estimates unrealistic
⇨ Objectives not clearly defined or measurable
⇨ Project manager: poor communication skills
⇨ Objectives changed during project
⇨ Project manager: poor leadership skills
⇨ Senior management: not showing strong support
⇨ Stakeholders: not taking ownership of the project
⇨ Role and responsibilities of the project team not defined
⇨ Resources not identified/made available at the start
⇨ Project team: did not work as a team

Study tip

Find some examples of real projects that have failed for these reasons

Definition

Strategy – a course of action, including the resources required, to achieve a specific objective

Scope – the extent of work needed to produce the project's deliverables

Project manager

Roles

⇨ Organising
⇨ Planning
⇨ Controlling

Skills

⇨ Leadership
⇨ Communication
⇨ Negotiation
⇨ Delegation
⇨ Problem solving
⇨ Change management

Study tip

Make sure that you are completely comfortable
with the roles and skills of the project manager
– it is likely to be examined frequently

Problems with teams

⇨ Unclear team goals and objectives
⇨ Lack of team structure
⇨ Lack of definition of roles
⇨ Poor leadership
⇨ Poor team communication
⇨ Lack of commitment

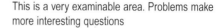

Watch out!

This is a very examinable area. Problems make more interesting questions

Stakeholders and matrix structures

⇨ Project sponsor
⇨ Project owner
⇨ Customers/users
⇨ Project manager
⇨ Project team
⇨ Suppliers

Matrix structure

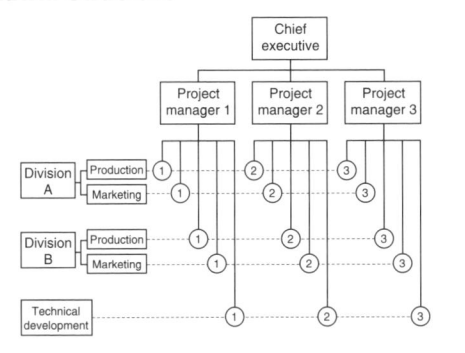

Advantages of matrix structure

⇨ Improved decision making
⇨ Direct contact rather than formal control
⇨ Good for management development
⇨ Improved coordination and communication
⇨ Balances customer/product needs with specialist expertise

Disadvantages of matrix structure

⇨ Lack of clear responsibility
⇨ Clash of priorities
⇨ Functional specialists may lose contact
⇨ Can limit career development
⇨ Employee confusion
⇨ Each member has two managers
⇨ Management time wasted in meetings

Project Management

Topics

- Project management process
- Feasibility study
- Costs
- Risk and uncertainty
- Risk management
- SWOT analysis
- Project plans
- Project constraints
- Gantt charts
- Network analysis
- PERT
- Project management software
- Performing and controlling the project
- Project management methodologies
- Post-completion review
- Continuous improvement

Key learning system questions

Project management process

Definition

Project management – the integration of all aspects of a project, ensuring that the proper knowledge and resources are available when and where needed, and above all to ensure that the expected outcome is produced in a timely, cost-effective manner

⇨ Initiating
⇨ Planning
⇨ Executing (leadership)
⇨ Controlling
⇨ Completing

Study tip

Make sure that you can explain each of these stages

Types of feasibility

⇨ Technical
⇨ Social and ecological
⇨ Business
⇨ Financial

Study tip

You are unlikely to be expected to carry out a financial evaluation of a project, but you must be able to explain each of the evaluation techniques

Costs

Types of cost

⇨ Capital
⇨ Revenue
⇨ Finance

Financial evaluation

⇨ Payback
⇨ Discounted cashflow (net present value or internal rate of return)
⇨ Accounting rate of return
⇨ Return on investment

Definitions

Risk – the probability of an undesirable event

Uncertainty – a situation where the probability of a contingent event is impossible to quantify

Types of risk

⇨ Quantitative
⇨ Socially constructed
⇨ Qualitative

Ranking qualitative risk

Potential scale or significance of loss		Low	Medium	High
	High	C	B	A
	Medium	D	C	B
	Low	E	D	C
		Low	Medium	High
			Likelihood	

Risk management

Steps

⇨ Identification
⇨ Analysis
⇨ Prioritisation
⇨ Management
⇨ Resolution
⇨ Monitoring

Risk management approaches

⇨ Avoidance
⇨ Transference
⇨ Reduction

Strengths	Weaknesses
· Things going well · Good things we have	· Things going badly · Things we don't have
Opportunities	**Threats**

· External events or trends
  that are good for us
	· External events or trends
	  that are bad for us

Project plans

A project has plans for

⇨ Project authorisation
⇨ Time
⇨ Cost
⇨ Quality

And possibly for:

⇨ Resources
⇨ Contingency
⇨ Communication

Stages in planning

⇨ Divide the project into work packages
⇨ Estimate time and resources
⇨ Make a cost estimate
⇨ Portray the activities graphically (network analysis)
⇨ Carry out risk analysis
⇨ Calculate a project schedule and budget

Project Initiation Document (PID)

⇨ Background
⇨ Scope
⇨ Objectives
⇨ Approach
⇨ Deliverables
⇨ Exclusions
⇨ Constraints
⇨ Interfaces
⇨ Assumptions
⇨ Structure
⇨ Manager and team
⇨ Communication plan
⇨ Controls

Project constraints

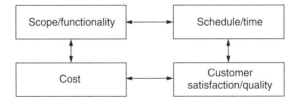

Gantt charts

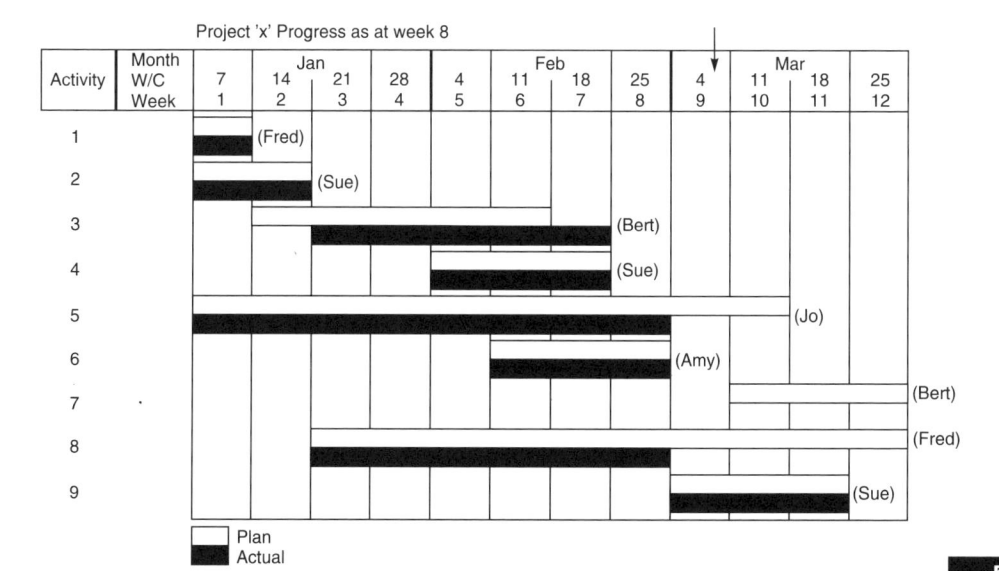

Project 'x' Progress as at week 8

Activity	Month W/C Week											

Plan

Actual

Network analysis

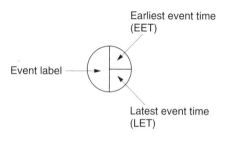

Event label ─── Earliest event time (EET)

Latest event time (LET)

Network elements

⇨ EET – earliest time at which any subsequent event can start

⇨ LET – the latest time at which all preceding activities must have been completed to prevent the whole project being delayed

⇨ Critical path – the series of events that must be completed as planned in order for the project to be completed on time

⇨ Elapsed time – the sum of the durations on the critical path (the planned duration of the whole project)

Study tip

You need to be able to explain and draw network diagrams. Make sure that you practise lots of questions

A completed network (activity on arrow)

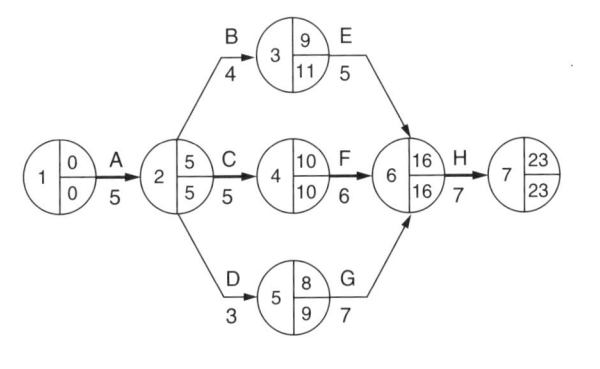

Activity on node method

Task/Activity, e.g. A, B, C, etc.	
Identity number of the activity	Duration of the activity
Earliest start time	Latest start time

A completed network (activity on node)

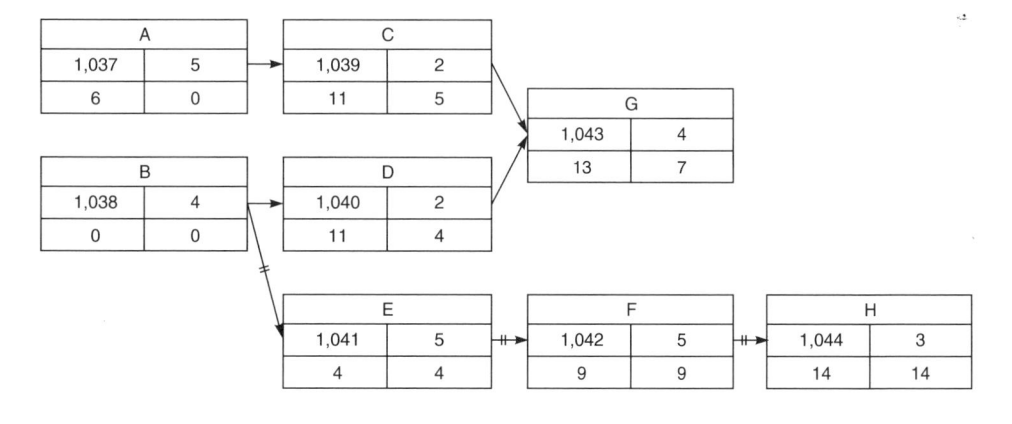

Definition

PERT – Project evaluation and review technique – a methodology for completing network analysis which reflects risk

Expected time

$$\frac{o + 4m + p}{6}$$

Contingency allowance

$$\frac{p - o}{6}$$

Definition

Milestone – An event that is clearly identifiable as a measure of how far the project has progressed, and how far it has to run

Definition

Control gate – A key point in the project life cycle which gives the project sponsor or steering committee an opportunity to review project progress, and make a decision whether to proceed further or to terminate the project

Project management software

Functions

⇨ Budgeting and cost control
⇨ Calendars
⇨ Graphics
⇨ Multiple project handling
⇨ Planning (work breakdown, network/CPA)
⇨ Scheduling (Gantt chart)
⇨ Resource planning
⇨ Resource histograms
⇨ Reporting

Advantages

⇨ Accuracy
⇨ Affordability
⇨ Ease of use
⇨ Ability to handle complexity
⇨ Speed
⇨ 'What if' analysis
⇨ Timesheet recording

Problems

⇨ Emphasis on plan, not project
⇨ Mythical man-month
⇨ Estimates
⇨ Skills
⇨ Work breakdown

Performing and controlling the project

⇨ Initiating
⇨ Planning
⇨ Executing leadership
⇨ Controlling
⇨ Completing

Need to determine

⇨ The major work elements
⇨ The resources required
⇨ A time estimate

Controlling the project

⇨ Monitor performance
⇨ Compare to plan
⇨ Report deviations
⇨ Impleme nt corrective action

Study tip

Make sure that you can explain each of these stages

PRINCE2

⇨ Clear structure of authority and responsibility
⇨ Management products
⇨ Different types of plan
⇨ Quality controls

Other methodologies

⇨ IDEAL
⇨ PMBoK
⇨ Six Sigma

Study tip

You do not need to know the detail of any specific methodology, but PRINCE2 will be used for illustration by the examiner

Key PRINCE2 processes

⇨ Directing the project
⇨ Planning a project
⇨ Starting up a project
⇨ Initiating a project
⇨ Controlling a stage
⇨ Managing product delivery
⇨ Managing the stage boundaries
⇨ Closing a project

Post-completion review

Stages of post-completion audit

⇨ Extent to which quality has been achieved
⇨ Efficiency of the solution vs. plan
⇨ Actual cost vs. budgeted cost
⇨ Time taken vs. plan
⇨ Effectiveness of the management process
⇨ Problems and solutions

The project management maturity model

⇨ Level 1 – common knowledge
⇨ Level 2 – common processes
⇨ Level 3 – singular methodology
⇨ Level 4 – benchmarking
⇨ Level 5 – continuous improvement

Management

Topics

- Key definitions
- Leadership and management
- Theories of management
- Organisational culture

Key definitions

Definitions

Power – the ability to exert an influence

Authority – the right to exercise power

Responsibility – the expectation of being held to account for success or failure

Delegation – the passing of authority and work to a subordinate

Sources of power

⇨ Reward power
⇨ Coercive power
⇨ Referent power
⇨ Expert power
⇨ Legitimate power

Study tip

These definitions are tricky. Make sure you can explain each term and the differences between the concepts

Leadership and management

Personality traits

⇨ Impulse
⇨ Integrity
⇨ Self-awareness
⇨ Human sympathy
⇨ Tough-mindedness

Management styles (Lewin)

⇨ Democratic
⇨ Laissez-faire
⇨ Authoritarian

Leadership and management

Management styles (Likert)

⇨ Exploitive-authoritative
⇨ Benevolent-authoritative
⇨ Consultative
⇨ Participative

Management styles (Blake & Mouton)

⇨ Country club
⇨ Middle-of-the-road
⇨ Authority-compliance
⇨ Impoverished
⇨ Team

Management styles (Tannenbaum & Schmidt)

⇨ Tells
⇨ Sells
⇨ Consults
⇨ Joins

Theories of management

Scientific management (Taylor)

⇨ Developed a science of work
⇨ Used science to select and develop staff
⇨ Prompted the mental revolution
⇨ Introduced cooperation and consultation
⇨ Introduced specialisation

Scope of management (Fayol)

⇨ Planning
⇨ Organising
⇨ Coordinating
⇨ Commanding
⇨ Controlling

Principles of management (Fayol)

⇨ Division of labour
⇨ Authority and responsibility
⇨ Discipline
⇨ Unity of command
⇨ Unity of direction
⇨ Personal interest
⇨ Remuneration
⇨ Scalar chain
⇨ Material and social order
⇨ Equity
⇨ Stability of tenure
⇨ Esprit de corps
⇨ Initiative
⇨ Centralisation

Theories of management

Motivational factors (Herzberg)

⇨ Challenging tasks
⇨ Achievement
⇨ Responsibility
⇨ Personal growth
⇨ Advancement
⇨ Recognition

Hygiene factors (Herzberg)

⇨ Rules
⇨ Environment
⇨ Work breaks
⇨ Supervision
⇨ Wages and benefits

Bureaucracy (Weber)

⇨ Specialisation
⇨ Hierarchy
⇨ Rules
⇨ Impersonality
⇨ Appointed officials
⇨ Career officials
⇨ Full-time officials
⇨ Public/private division

Watch out!

Bureaucracy is not necessarily bad. At the time of Weber's work it was clearly preferable to the sort of chaos that then constituted management in most organisations

Burns and Stalker

Mechanistic organisation

⇨ Task specialisation
⇨ Clear definitions of authority
⇨ Coordination and communication
⇨ Emphasis on hierarchy
⇨ Local recruitment

Organic organisation

⇨ Skills recognised as valuable
⇨ Integration of effort
⇨ Consultative leadership
⇨ Commitment to task
⇨ Variety of employee sources

Study tip

All this management theory can seem a bit tricky, but it's just different groups of writers trying to understand why different organisations work in different ways. In an examination question, just take a contingency approach and 'steal' the most appropriate parts from each theory

Theories of management

Managing in different cultures (Hofstede)

⇨ Power distance
⇨ Uncertainty avoidance
⇨ Individualism/collectivism
⇨ Masculinity/femininity
⇨ Time orientation

Cultural factors

⇨ Language
⇨ Religion
⇨ Attitudes
⇨ Social organisation
⇨ Education
⇨ Ethnocentrism

Study tip

Managing in different cultures is very topical, due to the growth in international and multinational organisations

Organisational culture

Definition

Culture – the way we do things round here

Study tip

Culture can be seen as the informal aspects of structure (see 'The Organisational Iceberg')

A strong culture will

⇨ Strengthen behaviour and norms
⇨ Minimise perceptual differences
⇨ Reflect the philosophy and values of the founder
⇨ Have a significant effect on strategy and responsiveness

Organisational culture

McKinsey 7-S framework

⇨ Systems
⇨ Structure
⇨ Style
⇨ Strategy
⇨ Staff
⇨ Skills
⇨ Shared values

Ouchi

⇨ Theory A
⇨ Theory J
⇨ Theory Z

Deal and Kennedy

⇨ Tough guy macho
⇨ Work hard, play hard
⇨ Bet your company
⇨ Process

Harrison

⇨ Power
⇨ Role
⇨ Task
⇨ Person

Peters and Waterman (the excellence principles)

⇨ A bias for action
⇨ Close to the customer
⇨ Autonomy and entrepreneurship
⇨ Productivity through people
⇨ Hands on, value driven
⇨ Stick to the knitting
⇨ Simple form, lean staff
⇨ Simultaneous loose–tight properties

Management of Working Relationships

Topics

- Group development
- Team roles
- Problems with groups
- Communication
- Meetings
- Managing the finance function
- Negotiation

Group development

Types of group

⇨ Reference group
⇨ Informal group
⇨ Formal group
⇨ Autonomous group

Study tip

Don't forget that organisations and project teams are examples of formal groups. That makes this theory very examinable

Group formation (Tuckman)

⇨ Forming
⇨ Storming
⇨ Norming
⇨ Performing

Factors affecting group integration

⇨ Homogeneity
⇨ Alternatives
⇨ Size
⇨ Other groups
⇨ Task
⇨ Isolation
⇨ Climate

Team roles

Team roles (Belbin)

⇨ Chairman
⇨ Shaper
⇨ Plant
⇨ Monitor-evaluator
⇨ Company worker
⇨ Resource investigator
⇨ Team worker
⇨ Completer-finisher
⇨ Expert

High performance work teams (Vaill)

⇨ Perform excellently against standard and past performance
⇨ Perform beyond what is thought to be their best
⇨ Are judged to be better than comparable groups
⇨ Achieve results with fewer resources than are thought necessary
⇨ Are seen to be exemplar of the culture

Study tip

You need to be able to identify these roles from a scenario

Problems with groups

Definition

Conformity – a member is pressured to conform, particularly to agree to decisions that are clearly wrong

The Abilene paradox – group members conform through silent acceptances and the belief that others support the behaviour

Groupthink – the homogeneity of objectives and thinking carried to the ultimate, and often disastrous extreme

Risky shift – the group seems willing to take decisions that are more risky than any member would take alone

Study tip

Each of these could form the topic of a question or requirement in the exam

Examples

⇨ Meetings
⇨ Telephone conversations
⇨ Videoconferencing
⇨ Memos
⇨ Email
⇨ Reports
⇨ Presentations

Study tip

Make sure that you are familiar with 'best practice' for each of these communication methods, and can identify when performance described in a scenario does not achieve it

Project meetings

⇨ Status review
⇨ Design review
⇨ Problem solving

Meeting roles

⇨ Chairperson
⇨ Facilitator
⇨ Secretary
⇨ Protagonists
⇨ Antagonists

Effective meetings

⇨ Determine the purpose
⇨ Establish attendance
⇨ Determine agenda
⇨ Make arrangements
⇨ Facilitate discussion
⇨ Manage action plan
⇨ Summarise
⇨ Publish minutes

Study tip

Watch out for questions relating to problems with
meetings

Managing the finance function

Definition

Business Process Outsourcing (BPO) –
Contracting with a third party (external supplier)
to provide part or all of a business process or
function. Many of these BPO efforts involve
offshoring

Definition

Offshoring – A type of outsourcing and simply
means having the outsourced business function
done in another country

Benefits

⇨ Cost reduction
⇨ Expertise
⇨ Release of capacity

Drawbacks

⇨ Loss of control
⇨ Risk to innovation
⇨ Risk to competitive advantage
⇨ Difficulty of managing

Negotiation

Phases

⇨ Preparation
⇨ Opening
⇨ Bargaining
⇨ Closing

Methods

⇨ Focus on objectives, not detail
⇨ Settle for what is fair
⇨ Listen and compromise
⇨ Trade-off wins and losses

Control Systems in Organisations

Topics

- Internal control
- Levels of control
- Health and safety at work
- Ethics
- Corporate governance

Internal control

Definition

Internal control – the whole system of controls, financial and otherwise, established by the management in order to carry on the business of the enterprise in an orderly and efficient manner, ensure adherence to management policies, safeguard the assets and secure as far as possible the completeness and accuracy of the records

Framework of control

⇨ Control environment
⇨ Control procedures

Control models

⇨ Feedback
⇨ Feedforward
⇨ Closed loop
⇨ Open loop
⇨ Double loop
⇨ Negative feedback
⇨ Positive feedback

Levels of control

⇨ Strategic
⇨ Tactical
⇨ Operational

Effectiveness

⇨ Acceptable
⇨ Appropriate
⇨ Accessible
⇨ Action-oriented
⇨ Adaptable
⇨ Affordable

Study tip

Make sure you have lots of examples of specific controls at each level

Health and safety at work

Employer obligations

➪ Risk-free equipment and systems of work
➪ Safety in use, storage, transport and handling
➪ Information, training, instruction and supervision
➪ Safe workplace
➪ Safe working environment

Safety issues

➪ Safety committee
➪ Managing safety
➪ Working with contractors
➪ Health and safety training
➪ Managing health
➪ Stress

Definition

Ethics – The distinction between what is considered 'right' and what is consider 'wrong' behaviour and with the way in which individuals arrive at such judgments in terms of moral duty and obligations that govern conduct

Factors affecting ethics (Carroll)

1. The categorical imperative
2. The conventionalist ethic
3. The golden rule
4. The hedonistic rule
5. The disclosure rule
6. The intuition rule
7. The means to an end ethic
8. The might equals right rule
9. The organisational ethics
10. The professional ethics
11. The utilitarian principle

Questions to ask

⇨ Is it legal?
⇨ Is it balanced?
⇨ Is it right?

The ethical organisation

⇨ Compliance-based
⇨ Integrity-based

Ethics

Different views

⇨ Profit motive
⇨ Natural purpose
⇨ Stakeholder view
⇨ Egotistical view

CIMA's ethical principles

1. Integrity
2. Objectivity
3. Professional Competence and Due Care
4. Confidentiality
5. Professional Behaviour

Threats

⇨ Self-interest threats
⇨ Self-review threats
⇨ Advocacy threats
⇨ Familiarity threats
⇨ Intimidation threats

Safeguards

⇨ Requirements for entry into the profession
⇨ Continuing professional development
⇨ Corporate governance regulations
⇨ Professional standards
⇨ Monitoring and disciplinary procedures
⇨ External review
⇨ Effective, well-publicised complaints systems
⇨ Duty to report breaches of ethical requirements

Corporate governance

Definition

Corporate governance – The system by which companies are directed and controlled

Treadway and COSO

⇨ Audit committee
⇨ Non-executive directors

Cadbury

⇨ Openness, integrity, accountability
⇨ Guidance on reporting
⇨ Audit procedures and report

Rutteman

⇨ Statement of directors' responsibilities

Greenbury

⇨ Directors' pay
⇨ Remuneration committee

Hampel

⇨ Produced the 'combined code'

Corporate governance

The combined code principles cover the following areas:
⇨ Directors
⇨ Remuneration
⇨ Shareholder relations
⇨ Accountability and audit

Study tip

Try to relate the corporate governance rules in these four areas to potential conflicts between stakeholders

Note that corporate governance was necessary because of conflicting objectives

Benefits

⇨ Reduces risk
⇨ Stimulates performance
⇨ Improves access to capital markets
⇨ Enhances marketability
⇨ Improves leadership
⇨ Demonstrates transparency

Conflict and Discipline

Topics

- Conflict
- Conflict symptoms
- Discipline
- Dismissal and redundancy
- Fairness

Conflict

Definition

Conflict – activity between groups or individuals that presumes direct interference with goal achievement

Characteristics

⇨ Diversion of energy
⇨ Altered judgement
⇨ Loser effects
⇨ Poor coordination

Conflict is caused by

⇨ Environment
⇨ Size
⇨ Technology
⇨ Goals
⇨ Structure
⇨ Goal incompatibility
⇨ Differentiation
⇨ Task interdependence
⇨ Uncertainty
⇨ Reward system

Conflict symptoms

You need to be able to identify the symptoms of conflict, and recommend how to deal with it. Remember that some degree of conflict may be tolerated or encouraged to achieve a better solution

⇨ Problems being delegated upwards
⇨ Hostility and jealousy between groups
⇨ Poor communications, vertically or horizontally
⇨ Widespread frustration at lack of progress
⇨ Problems polarised around people and personalities, rather than issues

Handling conflict (Thomas)

⇨ Competing
⇨ Collaborating
⇨ Compromising
⇨ Avoiding
⇨ Accommodating

Resolving conflict

⇨ Alter the context
⇨ Alter the issue
⇨ Alter the relationship
⇨ Alter the individuals

Managing conflict

⇨ Bargaining
⇨ Satisficing
⇨ Sequential attention
⇨ Priority setting
⇨ Confrontation
⇨ Third party consultation
⇨ Member rotation
⇨ Superordinate goals
⇨ Intergroup training

Discipline

Definition

Discipline – when the members of the enterprise follow goals or objectives sensibly without overt conflict and conduct themselves according to the standards of acceptable behaviour

Discipline problems

⇨ Poor timekeeping, lateness or absenteeism
⇨ Poor work
⇨ Breaking rules
⇨ Refusing work
⇨ Poor attitude

Disciplinary procedure

1. Informal talk
2. Verbal warning
3. Written warning
4. Disciplinary action

Resolving issues

⇨ Arbitration
⇨ Conciliation
⇨ Tribunals

Dismissal and redundancy

Valid reasons for dismissal

⇨ Conduct
⇨ Capability
⇨ Breach of statutory duty
⇨ Other substantial reason
⇨ Redundancy

Valid reasons for redundancy

⇨ Cessation of business
⇨ Relocation of business
⇨ Cessation of type of work

Fairness

Modern view

⇨ No expectation of lifetime contracts
⇨ Appropriate reward in line with contribution
⇨ Opportunity for career

Psychological contract

⇨ Coercive contract
⇨ Calculative contract
⇨ Cooperative contract

Other relevant legislation

⇨ Working time
⇨ Childcare

Diversity and equal opportunities

Equal opportunities	Diversity
Removing discrimination	Maximising potential
Issues for disadvantaged groups	Relevant to all employees
A personnel and development role	A managerial role
Relies on proactive action	Does not rely on proactive action